W9-AYA-615

HOCKEY
PLAY BY THE RULES

DAVID AND PATRICIA ARMENTROUT

796.962
ARM

Kennedy Library
77th & Central
Burbank, IL 60459

The Rourke Press, Inc.
Vero Beach, Florida 32964

© 1998 The Rourke Press, Inc.

All rights reserved. No part of this book may be reproduced or utilized in any form or by any means, electronic or mechanical including photocopying, recording, or by any information storage and retrieval system without permission in writing from the publisher.

Patricia and David Armentrout specialize in nonfiction writing and have had several book series published for primary schools. They reside in Cincinnati with their two children.

PROJECT EDITORS:
Dick Doughty is a former Elementary School teacher who now operates his own business. He coached hockey for 9 years from the minor level through Junior "A." Dick is a certified Level 3 OMHA referee and is currently Referee-in-Chief for his hometown minor hockey association.

Rob Purdy has been a Secondary School teacher for 16 years. He is a certified Advance I hockey coach and a NCCP coaching instructor. Rob has coached hockey for 10 years in the OMHA, with a Pee Wee championship in 1997.

PHOTO CREDITS:
all photos © Kim Karpeles except © East Coast Studios: page 4; © Craig Melvin/Allsport: page 27

REFEREE ILLUSTRATIONS:
Jim Spence

EDITORIAL SERVICES:
Penworthy Learning Systems

Library of Congress Cataloging-in-Publication Data

Armentrout, David, 1962-
    Hockey—play by the rules / David Armentrout, Patricia Armentrout.
       p. cm. — (Hockey)
    Includes index.
    Summary: Presents basic information about the game of hockey, with particular emphasis on its rules and regulations.
    ISBN 1-57103-221-5
    1. Hockey—Rules—Juvenile literature. [1. Hockey.] I. Armentrout, Patricia, 1960-
. II. Title.   III. Series: Armentrout, David, 1962-   Hockey.
QV847.5.A76 1998
796.962—dc21   98–27371
                                                                          CIP
                                                                          AC

Printed in the USA

TABLE OF CONTENTS

EXAMPLE OF ICING

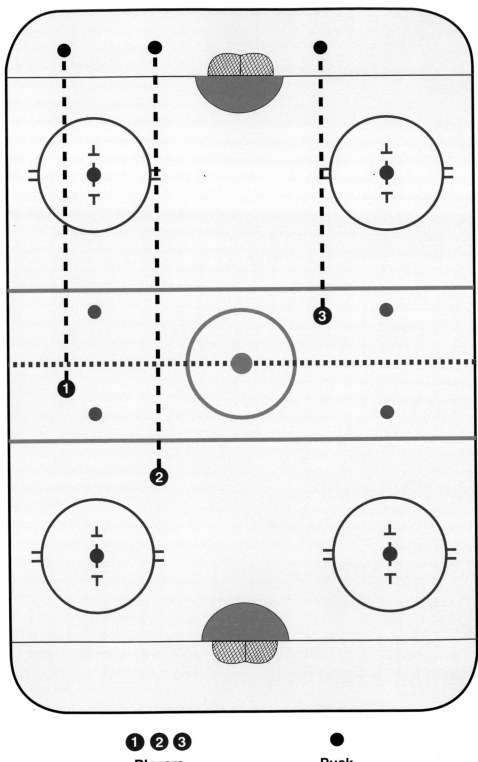

1 **2** **3**
Players

● **Puck**

Player 3, is the only player not icing.

4

CHAPTER ONE

HOCKEY RULES

Ice hockey is played by men and women, boys and girls, **amateurs** and **professionals**. They all play the same sport, but they don't all play by the same rules. The National Hockey League (NHL) has its own rules; the National Collegiate Athletic Association (NCAA) has its own hockey rules, and the list goes on. Most of the rules are similar, though, no matter which league you play in.

Why are some rules different? Adult games can be more physical and aggressive than youth games, because adults are bigger and stronger than children.

This is true in many sports. For example, young athletes play flag football, a form of football that does not allow tackling. Many children play whiffle ball, T-ball, and softball instead of baseball. Those games are geared to young players.

Players learn to play by different rules as they grow bigger, stronger, and more skilled. Playing in a **Junior Hockey** league, for example, gives players a chance to improve their hockey skills. They develop a style of play that prepares them for competition.

Most youth leagues across the United States follow the official rules of USA Hockey, Inc. Most youth leagues in Canada follow the official rules of the Canadian Hockey Association. All associations have printed material detailing their rules. For example, if your league plays by USA hockey rules, contact them for a copy.

The Game

An ice hockey game involves three 20-minute periods of play. An intermission follows the first and second period. USA Hockey rules allow each team to take a one-minute timeout per game during a stoppage of play (while play has stopped).

★ **DID YOU KNOW?**

A game has a starting line-up of players. Players fatigue quickly due to the nature of the game, so line changes will occur many times.

Youth hockey players are eager to learn the game.

A coach instructs players from the player's bench.

The Canadian Hockey Association permits each team to take a 30-second timeout per game.

The object of the game is to shoot the puck into the opponent's **goal**. Each goal is worth one point. The team with the most goals at the end of the third period is the winner. It is possible that there would be a tie score at the end of the third period. Most, but not all leagues, would play an additional 10-minute period—or go into overtime. The first team to score a goal is declared the winner. If no goal is scored the process can repeat.

Before the start of a game, a team designates a head coach and a team captain. The head coach is responsible for the team's actions before, during, and after the game. The captain, one of the team members, represents the team. The captain is the only player allowed to discuss with the referee, any questions during a game. Some leagues also have assistant captains. The team manager or coach gives the **referee** or the **official** scorer a list of eligible players who are to play in the game. Eighteen players plus two goalkeepers are allowed to play in a single game.

★ DID YOU KNOW?

One "goal" point is credited to the scoring record of a player who directs the puck into the opponent's goal. One "assist" point is credited to the scoring record of a player who takes part in the play immediately before a goal.

Each team begins a game with six players on the ice: three forwards (center, right wing and left wing), two defense players (left and right), and a goalkeeper.

Players draw a penalty if they break a rule. Three basic rules deal with passing the puck, scoring goals, and substituting players.

A player is allowed to pass the puck to a teammate within the same playing zone. A player is also allowed to pass to a teammate from the defensive zone into the neutral zone as long as the puck does not cross two lines.

It feels great to score a goal!

A referee calls a penalty near center ice.

A goal is scored when an attacking player shoots the puck with a stick and it crosses the opposing team's goal line and enters the net. If the puck deflects off a player before it crosses the goal line and enters the net, a goal is scored.

Players can be substituted while play is stopped or "on the fly," or during play. An on-the-fly change is allowed as long as the player leaving the ice gets to the players' bench before the replacement enters the ice. When a goalkeeper is changed, he or she must be within 10 feet (3 meters) of the players' bench before the replacement is allowed on the ice.

OFFICIALS

    Most organized team sports use officials to oversee the game. Officials make sure everyone is playing by the rules. Each official has certain responsibilities. Most hockey games use three on-ice officials—a referee and two **linesmen**. The officials wear ice hockey skates, official sweaters, black pants, and a black hockey helmet. Each is equipped with a whistle. The officials enter the ice before the warmup and stay until the end of each period, until all players have gone to their dressing rooms.

Other game officials include two goal judges, a penalty timekeeper, a game timekeeper, and an official scorer.

A referee supervises the games. The referee orders the teams on the ice before the game and before the start of each period. The referee has control over all other officials and the players before, during, and after a game. In disputes during a game, the referee's decision is the final decision.

The referee applies, or imposes, penalties in a game. If necessary, a referee talks with a linesman or a goal judge before deciding on a penalty. The referee announces to the official scorer and penalty timekeeper any penalties imposed on a player and any goals or assists that have been made.

The linesmen stop play for a rule **infraction**, such as icing, offside, or improper substituting. The linesmen do not impose penalties, but they report rule violations to the referee. The linesmen also conduct face-offs except at the start of a game, start of a period, and after a goal is scored.

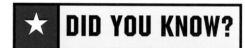 **DID YOU KNOW?**

The referee decides if a stick is unfit for normal play. If a player breaks a stick, he or she should drop it right away. Playing with a broken stick can be unsafe and results in a minor penalty.

Face-off opponents focus on the puck.

Two opposing wingers await the outcome of the face-off.

A goal judge sits in a screened area behind each team's goal. A goal judge decides whether the puck has passed between the two goal posts, under the crossbar, and over the goal line. A goal judge decides "goal" or "no goal."

A penalty timekeeper keeps all records of players who serve penalties. The record shows the type of penalty and the amount of time. A penalty timekeeper also ensures that penalties are posted correctly on the scoreboard.

A game timekeeper signals the referee to start a game; gives a 3-minute warning before the second and third periods; and signals the referee to start those periods. A game timekeeper also has the last minute in each period announced over the public address system.

An official scorer keeps records of all goals scored and all players who score or assist on goals. An official scorer also records the time when a temporary or substitute goalkeeper enters the ice. An official scorer prepares a score sheet that the referee signs at the end of a game.

★ **DID YOU KNOW?**

A goalkeeper is allowed to play with a broken stick until a normal stop in play. A goalkeeper cannot get a replacement stick from the players' bench; a teammate must do it for the goalie.

Who Officiates and Why?

Just about anyone—ages 11 to 70—can become a hockey official. They are students, parents, and even hockey players.

Players officiate to learn more about the rules of the game and to spend more time on the ice. Ex-players officiate to stay involved in the game. Parents officiate because they like to be involved in their children's sporting events. Students officiate to earn money. They all officiate because they love ice hockey!

The referee watches the play from behind the goal.

A face-off starts when an official drops the puck between two opposing players.

USA Hockey has a program for preparing officials. Before officiating at games, you would need to register, pay an annual fee, and pass an open-book exam on hockey rules. Officials attend training camps and workshops to improve their skills.

Depending on an official's skill level and experience, he or she can officiate games at four levels. Officials registered with USA Hockey officiate games and tournaments from youth level to Olympic level.

Officials spend as much, or more time on the ice in a game as the players. They also train as much as the players to stay in top physical condition. They must be fast, agile, and have a quick eye for staying on top of the game.

CHAPTER THREE

PENALTIES

Serving a penalty means "doing time." A player who violates a rule is penalized and sent to the penalty box. The penalty box is usually a bench, one for each team, alongside the neutral zone. The amount of time spent in the penalty box depends on the violation. In some cases, a penalty can be a **penalty shot** awarded to the opponent.

All penalties are classified as one of six types: **minor penalty, bench minor penalty, major penalty, misconduct penalty, match penalty,** and penalty shot.

Certain rules apply to penalties. For example, when a player on the visiting team is penalized for the same violation as a home-team player, the visiting player must go to the penalty box first. Also, if a violation occurs when play is not in progress, such as during a warmup, a penalty can still be imposed.

A minor penalty is imposed on a player (except a goalkeeper) who violates a rule while on the ice. The player is ruled off the ice for 2 minutes and no substitution can be made. A player may leave the penalty box before the 2 minutes are up if the opposing team scores while the player is in the box.

A bench minor penalty is given to a player who violates a rule while off the ice during a game. A bench minor penalty lasts 2 minutes and no substitution can be made. Any player can serve a bench minor penalty—it doesn't have to be the player who made the infraction. A team's manager or coach chooses a player on the ice to serve the penalty.

★ DID YOU KNOW?

A team is considered shorthanded when the opposing team has more players on the ice due to penalties.

After serving a 2-minute penalty, this player can now get back into the game.

The goalie tries to block the puck.

Major penalties are more serious. A player is ruled off the ice for 5 minutes and must remain in the penalty box the entire time, even if the opposing team scores a goal. If a second major penalty is imposed on the same player during the same game, he or she also draws a game misconduct penalty.

A misconduct penalty means a player is removed from the game for 10 minutes, but a player substitution is allowed. A game misconduct penalty means a player is suspended from the rest of the game, but a substitution is allowed. A player can be suspended from the team's next two games for drawing a game misconduct penalty.

A match penalty means a player is ruled off the ice for the rest of the game and ordered to the dressing room immediately. At the same time, a teammate must sit in the penalty box for 5 minutes. (Note: Substitution is permitted if the other team is imposed with the same match penalty.) A match penalty is usually assessed for breaking the intent-to-injure rule.

★ **DID YOU KNOW?**

A goal may be awarded to an attacking team if the defending team deliberately displaces the goal post, keeping the puck out of the goal. It needs to be obvious to the referee that the puck would have entered the goal.

The penalty shot gives an advantage to the penalized player's opponent, instead of taking time away from the rule-breaking player. A player is allowed to skate alone towards the goalkeeper and try to score a goal. Other players must remain behind the red center line and along the sides of the rink. The penalty shot begins at the center ice spot and is considered complete as soon as the shot is taken. If a goal is scored, play resumes with a face-off at center ice. If no goal is scored, then play is resumed with a face-off at a face-off spot in the zone where the penalty shot was attempted.

A player may receive a minor penalty for hooking.

Unsportsmanlike conduct in an NHL game.

Kennedy Library
77th & Central
Burbank, IL 60459

Two more playing rules that will help you understand the game involve "icing the puck" and "offsides." Icing occurs when a player shoots the puck from the team's half of the ice beyond the opponent's goal line (but not in front of the net). Icing gives the defending team a brief advantage because play is stopped and a face-off is held in the offending team's zone.

The offside rule states that no player on the attacking team can skate ahead of, or precede, the puck into the attacking zone. Any player doing so is considered "offside." If this rule is violated, play is stopped and a face-off follows.

If a defending player is able to play the puck near or at the blue line and pass or carry (by stickhandling) the puck into the neutral zone, then the offside violation does not apply. This situation is called a delayed offside.

SPORTSMANSHIP

Body contact between opponents occurs naturally during the course of a hockey game. Hockey, as sometimes seen in adult games, has a reputation for being too physical. For this reason, managers and coaches of youth hockey stress the fundamental skills and enjoyment of the sport, rather than competition and winning.

Hockey puts 12 people on the ice with sticks in hand to scramble for a small disk. So, of course it's going to be physical!

Just because a game is physical doesn't mean players can get away with unsportsmanlike conduct. Coaches and managers stress the importance of **sportsmanship**. Sportsmanship means playing fairly and losing gracefully. It also means respecting the officials and other players on the ice.

Unapproved behavior includes arguing with an official, throwing a stick or other object onto the ice, and shooting the puck after the whistle is blown. More serious violations include head-butting, fighting, and bad language. These actions lead to misconduct or game misconduct penalties.

Some rule infractions are not considered an act of misconduct. For example, tripping is a violation of a rule; but sometimes a player accidentally trips over another player. Accidental trips are not penalized, but a minor penalty will be imposed on a player who places his or her stick, foot, or arm in the way of an opponent, causing them to trip or fall.

Although youth hockey games are less competitive than games played in the higher ranks, young athletes still need clear rules and penalties. Some rule violations are explained on the next three pages. Other penalties and their signals are explained in chapter 5.

★ **DID YOU KNOW?**

Goalkeepers are not sent to the penalty bench for minor, major, or misconduct penalties. Another player from the same team serves the penalty for the goalkeeper.

Hockey is a tough, physical game.

A minor penalty may be imposed for carrying a stick above
normal height.

Violations

Body-checking is part of the game and is allowed as long as it is done right. To be legal, a player uses his or her trunk (not the head or limbs) to check an opponent between the knees and neck. Board-checking is allowed, but it is up to the referee to decide the degree of violence involved in a check. Checking from behind is not allowed and can be treated as an attempt to injure an opponent. A crosscheck occurs when a player who has both hands on the stick and no part of the stick on the ice checks another player. If a player is injured because of a crosscheck, a major penalty plus a game misconduct penalty are imposed.

The puck must be kept in motion at all times. Some rules include falling on the puck, handling the puck, and freezing the puck. A player may not fall on the puck to hold or stop it.

A player is not allowed to hold the puck in his or her hand. If a player handles the puck but drops it immediately, play will continue; otherwise, play will stop and a face-off will follow.

★ **DID YOU KNOW?**

A goalkeeper drawing a game misconduct penalty or match penalty is ordered off the ice and replaced with another goalkeeper or other player from his or her team. The goalkeeper who violated the rules may have to give up equipment to the replacement goalkeeper.

A goalkeeper cannot hold the puck for more than 3 seconds. Players may not "freeze" the puck along the boards. Freezing the puck can result in a minor penalty for delaying the game.

Several rules relate to use of the hockey stick. High-sticking, slashing, and hooking are among them. High-sticking is carrying the stick above the shoulders.

A legal board check.

Opposing teams show sportsmanship by shaking hands after a game.

Slashing is swinging a stick in the direction of another player. Hooking means using a stick blade to get in the way of an opponent's progress. These violations will get you a minor or major penalty. If these actions injure an opponent, a major penalty and game misconduct penalty are certain.

Spearing is another stick violation. Spearing occurs when a player stabs or attempts to stab an opponent with the blade of the stick. Just the spearing motion is a violation. Spearing always draws a major penalty plus a game misconduct penalty. Sometimes players become angry and frustrated during a game. This may cause them to lose their temper and commit a violation. These violations can sometimes mean the difference between winning or losing a game.

Rules and penalties for breaking them help make ice hockey a challenging, fun and safe sport.

OFFICIAL SIGNALS

Hockey officials work hard, just like the players. They skate up and down the rink watching for rule violations. They are able to recognize a violation as soon as it occurs. To do so the officials must know everything about the way a hockey game is played. Officials must know every rule inside and out.

Play is fast. Players move quickly, and constantly change from offense to defense and back again. Needless to say, not every violation is seen and penalized.

When you're watching a game, how do you know when a player breaks a rule? When you see a player enter the penalty box, you know a rule has been broken. How can you tell what happened and what penalty was given? One way, is to keep an eye on the referee and linesmen during a game. They use hand signals to describe rule violations. Also, you can look at the scoreboard. The penalty timekeeper makes sure the correct penalties are posted there.

Signals and What They Mean

Over 20 signals are used in ice hockey. The officials use an open hand for some signals, a closed fist for others. Sometimes an official blows a whistle along with hand and arm movements. Often the movement in the signal looks like the movement in the infraction. Not every signal means a rule infraction. It may mean a goal has been scored. The next few pages give examples of official signals and penalties.

When a goal is scored, an official blows a whistle and points directly at the goal.

A delayed, or slow, whistle signals a blue-line offside. The official puts a hand straight above his or her head.

★ **DID YOU KNOW?**

A referee uses a hand signal to signal a scored goal. A goal judge signals a goal with a red light.

CHARGING

INTERFERENCE

CROSSCHECKING

SLASHING

**TIMEOUT OR
UNSPORTSMANLIKE CONDUCT**

HIGH-STICKING

HOOKING

HOLDING

FIGHTING (ROUGHING)

ELBOWING

PENALTY SHOT

GOAL SCORED

If a player from the defending team is able to play the puck near the blue-line, the official drops the arm to cancel the offside call as soon as the puck is brought over the blue line and the offensive players clear the zone.

When the puck is shot and icing may have occurred, the back linesman signals the one in front, using the slow whistle signal. If icing is found, the front linesman gives the slow whistle signal to stop play. The back linesman then gives the icing signal—folded arms across the chest.

When a player uses an elbow to check an opponent, an official taps his or her own elbow.

When a player uses a knee to check an opponent, an official taps the right knee once with the right hand, while both skates remain on the ice.

Holding an opponent results in a minor penalty. To signal holding, an official clasps the wrist of the whistle hand as it is extended in front of the chest.

Grabbing or holding a player's face mask results in a major penalty plus a game misconduct penalty. To signal this infraction, an official holds a closed fist in front of the face, palm in, and pulls the arm straight down.

★ **DID YOU KNOW?**

Rule infractions that may injure players include the following actions: boarding, charging, checking from behind, crosschecking, elbowing and kneeing, high-sticking, roughing (fighting), and slashing.

A violation called "boarding" occurs when a player pushes an opponent into the boards, or walls, around the rink. An official strikes a closed fist into an open palm to signal boarding.

When a player uses the shaft of a hockey stick to jab or try to jab an opponent, the violation is called "butt-ending." An official signals it by moving a closed-fist forearm under an open-hand, palm-down forearm.

In U.S. hockey, an official places one bent arm behind the back to signal checking from behind. In Canadian hockey, an official extends both arms out in front with palms open.

Officials must learn over 20 signals.

A player enters the penalty box.

An official signals delaying the game by placing a hand, palm open, in front of the chest; then extends it forward.

An official signals spearing with one forward jab motion with both hands in front of the chest.

The signal for timeout and unsportsmanlike conduct is the same. An official, using both hands, forms a "T."

When a player deliberately trips an opponent, an official strikes the side of his or her knee once while both skates remain on the ice.

An official signals an act of misconduct by placing both hands on the hips.

Knowing basic ice hockey rules, penalties, and signals will help you understand and enjoy the game. Some U.S. and Canadian rules and signals differ slightly. Detailed information can be found in the rule books of USA Hockey, Inc, and the Canadian Hockey Association.

GLOSSARY

amateurs (AM uh terz) — people who play a sport without pay

bench minor penalty (BENCH MY nur PEN ul tee) — punishment for breaking a hockey rule while off the ice during a game; results in a player's removal from the ice for 2 minutes to serve the penalty

body-checking (BAHD ee CHEK ing) — using the hips or shoulders to throw off an opponent who is in possession of the puck

goal (GOL) — one-point score added to a team's record when a player shoots the puck across the opponent's goal line, between the goal posts, under the crossbar, and into the net; also the entire net and goal post framework

infraction (in FRAK shun) — the act of or an example of breaking a rule

Junior Hockey (JOON yer HAHK ee) — USA Hockey leagues for male hockey players ages 16 to 20

linesmen (LYNZ men) — trained on-ice officials who call offside and icing infractions, assist the referee in calling rule violations, and handle face-offs

major penalty (MAY jur PEN ul tee) — punishment for breaking a rule that results in a player being removed from the ice for 5 minutes

match penalty (MATCH PEN ul tee) — a punishment for breaking a rule that results in a player being removed from a game

GLOSSARY

minor penalty (MY nur PEN ul tee) — a punishment for breaking a rule that results in a player being removed from the ice for 2 minutes

misconduct penalty (mis KAHN dukt PEN ul tee) — a punishment for breaking a rule that results in a player being removed from the ice for 10 minutes

official (uh FISH ul) — person trained in hockey rules who supervises some part of games, such as (on ice) *referee*, who calls rule violations and imposes penalties, and *linesman* who calls rule infractions; also (off-ice) goal *judges*, *penalty timekeeper*, *game timekeeper*, and *scorer*.

penalty shot (PEN ul tee SHAHT) — a shot awarded to an offensive player who, while in control of the puck, misses a chance to score because of interference from an opposing player

professional (pruh FESH uh nul) — someone paid to participate in a sport

referee (REF eh REE) — a trained on-ice official who supervises games, calls violations and penalties, determines if goals are scored, and handles face-offs

sportsmanship (SPAWRT mun SHIP) — attitude and behavior suitable to hockey players; includes following rules, acting politely while playing to win, working hard, and losing gracefully

FURTHER READING

Find out more with these helpful books and information sites:

Harris, Lisa. *Hockey How to Play the All-Star Way,* Raintree Steck-Vaughn Publishers, 1994

Davidson, John, with John Steinbreder, *Hockey For Dummies An Official Publication of the NHL,* IDG Books Worldwide, Inc., 1997

USA Hockey *Official Rules Of Ice Hockey,* Triumph Books, 1997

Official Rule Book of the Canadian Hockey Association, Canadian Hockey Association, 1997

Amateur Hockey Online Ice Hockey Rules at www.ll.net/aho/ah-rules.htm

Canadian Hockey Association at www.canadianhockey.ca/

National Hockey League at www.nhl.com

USA Hockey, Inc. at www.usahockey.com

INDEX